Crazy Monster Trucks

Hot Rod Readers

Craig A. Lopetz

TABLE OF CONTENTS

A Crabtree Seedlings Book

CRABTREE
Publishing Company
www.crabtreebooks.com

What Are Crazy Monster Trucks?

Crazy monster trucks are **artist** drawings.

Some are drawn with **airbrush** paints.

Some are drawn on a computer.

Some crazy monster trucks
jump high.

Crazy monster trucks **crush** cars.

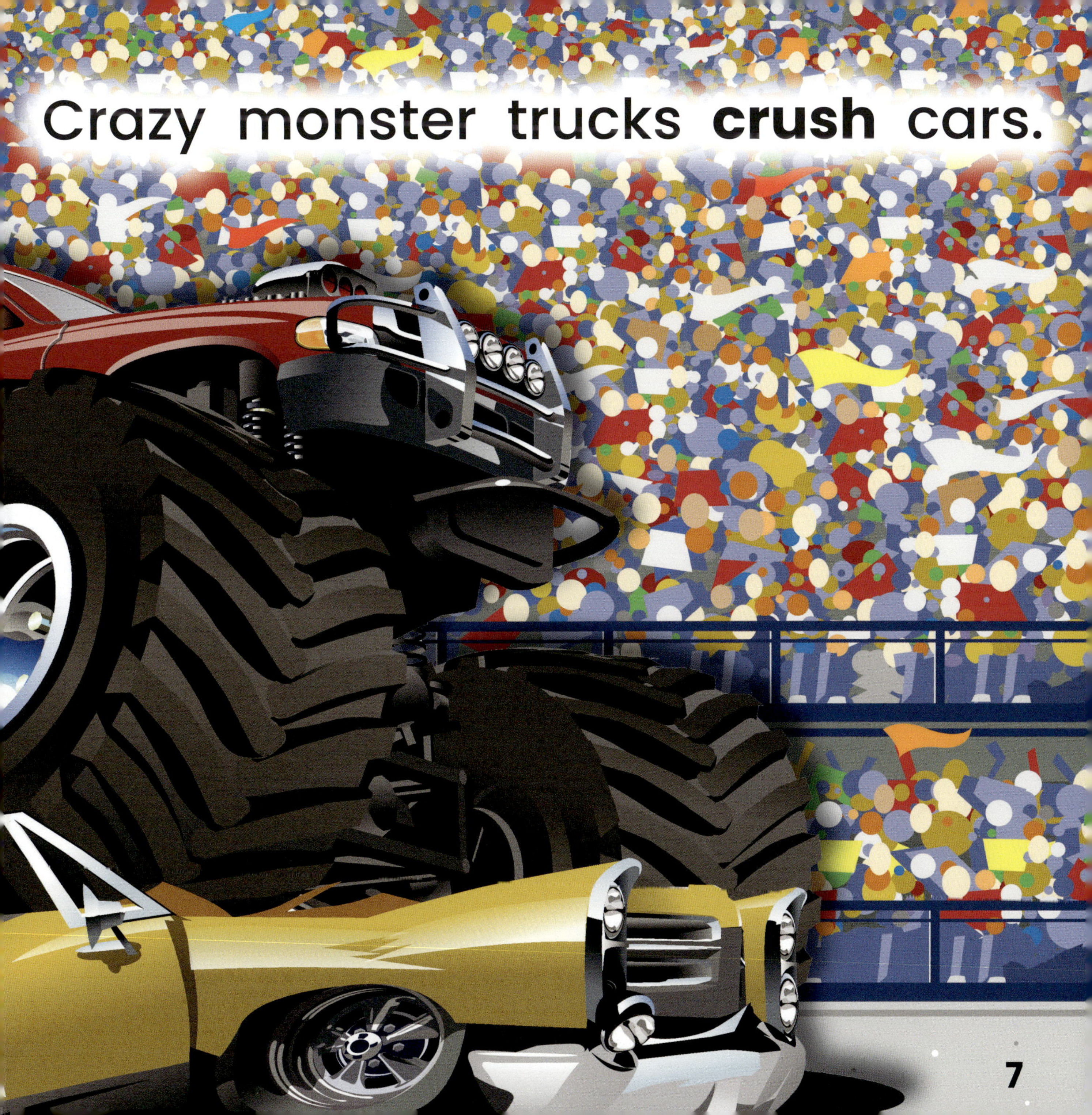

Crazy monster trucks have big, black tires.

Crazy monster trucks have big **motors.**

All monster trucks like mud!

Some crazy monster trucks are monster cars.

Crazy monster jeeps can drive in sand.

Crazy monster trucks move fast in the snow.

Some crazy monster trucks are made for work.

Crazy monster trucks are really cool!

Glossary

airbrush (AIR-brush): An airbrush is a tool that sprays paint.

artist (AR-tist): An artist is someone who is very good at drawing, painting, or making things.

crush (KRUSH): When you crush something, you press, squeeze, or squish it into pieces or a different shape.

motors (MOH-turz): Car motors are engines, or machines, that give cars their power.

Index

School-to-Home Support for Caregivers and Teachers

This book helps children grow by letting them practice reading. Here are a few guiding questions to help the reader build his or her comprehension skills. Possible answers appear here in red.

Before Reading

- **What do I think this book is about?** I think this book is about crazy big monster trucks. I think this book is about artists who draw crazy monster trucks.
- **What do I want to learn about this topic?** I want to learn more about how I could learn to draw crazy trucks. I want to learn more about the materials I will need to draw crazy trucks.

During Reading

- **I wonder why...** I wonder why people go to stadiums to watch monster trucks crush cars. I wonder why the tires are so large on crazy monster trucks.
- **What have I learned so far?** I have learned that crazy monster jeeps can drive fast in sand. I have learned that crazy monster trucks have very large black tires.

After Reading

- **What details did I learn about this topic?** I have learned that artists use an airbrush or a computer to draw crazy monster trucks. I have learned that some crazy monster trucks crush cars.
- **Read the book again and look for the glossary words.** I see the word *crush* on page 7, and the word *motors* on page 10. The other glossary words are found on page 23.

Library and Archives Canada Cataloguing in Publication

CIP available at Library and Archives Canada

Library of Congress Cataloging-in-Publication Data

CIP available at Library of Congress

Crabtree Publishing Company
www.crabtreebooks.com 1–800–387–7650

Written by: Craig A. Lopetz
Print coordinator: Katherine Berti

Print book version produced jointly with Blue Door Education in 2023

Printed in the U.S.A./072022/CG20220201

PHOTO CREDITS:
All images: www.istock.com: mechanick - Illustrator.

Published in the United States
Crabtree Publishing
347 Fifth Ave.
Suite 1402-145
New York, NY 10016

Published in Canada
Crabtree Publishing
616 Welland Ave.
St. Catharines, Ontario
L2M 5V6